A REOPAGITICA

A *Speech* of Mr. John Milton
for the Liberty of Unlicensed Printing,
to the Parliament of England

LONDON,
PRINTED IN THE YEAR 1644

τοὐλεύθερον δ'ἐκεῖνο · τίς θέλει πόλει
χρηστόν τι βούλευμ' ἐς μέσον φέρειν ἔχων;
καὶ ταῦθ ὁ χρῇζων λαμπρὸς ἔσθ', ὁ μὴ θέλων
σιγᾷ · τί τούτων ἔστ' ἰσαίτερον πόλει;

This is true liberty, when freeborn persons,
Having to advise the public, may speak freely,
And hu who can and will, deserves high praise;
Who neither can nor will, may hold hus peace;
What can be juster in a State than this?
Euripides, *The Suppliants*

BANDANNA BOOKS•1992•SANTA BARBARA

LITTLE HUMANIST CLASSICS

N O N S E X I S T • S E C U L A R

series editor, A.S. Ash

Second printing
LC 86-064056

ISBN 0-942208-04-8

EDITOR'S NOTE

Milton's essay on freedom of the press is one of the cornerstones of modern democracy. His survey of censorship shows the power of what was once known as a liberal education. John Milton was knowledgeable, thorough, yet driven by a passion for the life of the human spirit, and in the *Areopagitica* (named after the Areopagus, or Hill of Ares, where the tribunal met ancient Athens), he breathes new energy into old ideas, and makes anew the case for freedom of the mind.

I have elected to eliminate footnotes in this edition, to allow Milton's rhetoric to flow full force. The two tasks of editing unique to this edition are modernization and humanization. *Hath* must go, *unwillingest* becomes *most unwilling, while let no man* and *manhood* become *let no one* and *adulthood.* I also follow the practice of this Little Humanist Classics series in introducing the humanist pronouns HU, HUS, and HUM wherever the reference is to a third person generally, without reference to sex. *Hu, hus, hum* are pronounced exactly the same as the indefinite pronouns *who, whose, whom.*

A.S. Ash
January 1992

AREOPAGITICA

THEY WHO TO STATES AND governors of the Commonwealth direct their speech, High Court of Parliament, or, wanting such access in a private condition, write that which they foresee may advance the public good; I suppose them, as at the beginning of no mean endeavor, not a little altered and moved inwardly in their minds—some with doubt of what will be the success, others with fear of what will be the censure; some with hope, others with confidence of what they have to speak. And me perhaps each of these dispositions, as the subject was whereon I entered, may have at other times variously affected; and likely might in these foremost expressions now also disclose which of them swayed most, but that the very attempt of this address thus made, and the thought of whom it has recourse to, has got the power within me to a passion far more welcome than incidental to a preface.

Which though I stay not to confess before any ask, I shall be blameless, if it be no other than the joy and gratulation which it brings to all who wish and promote their country's liberty; whereof this whole discourse proposed will be a certain testimony, if not a trophy. For this is not the liberty which we can hope, that no grievance ever should arise in the Commonwealth—that let no one in this world expect; but when complaints are freely heard, deeply considered, and speedily reformed, then is the utmost bound of civil liberty attained that wise persons look for. To which, if I now manifest by the very sound of this which I shall utter, that we are already in good part arrived, and yet from such a steep disadvantage of tyranny and superstition grounded into our principles as was beyond the adulthood of a Roman recovery; it will be attributed first, as is most due, to the strong assistance of God our deliverer, next, to your faithful guidance and undaunted wisdom, Lords and Commons of England.

Neither is it in God's esteem the diminution of hus glory, when honorable things are spoken of good people and worthy magistrates; which if I now first should begin to do, after so fair a progress of your laudable deeds and such a long obligement upon the whole realm to your indefatigable virtues, I might be justly reckoned among the tardiest and the most unwilling of them that praise you.

Nevertheless, there being three principal things without which all praising is but courtship and flattery: first, when that only is praised which is solidly worth praise; next, when greatest likelihoods are brought that such things are truly and really in those persons to whom they are ascribed; the other, when hu who praises, by showing that such hus actual persuasion is of whom hu writes, can demonstrate that hu flatters not; the former two of these I have heretofore endeavored, rescuing the employment from hum who went about to impair your merits with a trivial and malignant encomium; the latter, as belonging chiefly to my own acquittal, that whom I so extolled I did not flatter, has been reserved opportunely to this occasion. For hu who freely magnifies what has been nobly done, and fears not to declare as freely what might be done better, gives you the best covenant of hus fidelity; and that hus loyalest affection and hus hope waits on your proceedings. Hus highest praising is not flattery, and hus plainest advice is a kind of praising; for though I should affirm and hold by argument that it would fare better with truth, with learning, and the Commonwealth, if one of your published orders, which I should name, were called in; yet at the same time it could not but much redound to the luster of your mild and equal government, whenas private persons are hereby animated to think you better pleased with public advice than other statists have been delighted heretofore with public flattery. And people will then see what difference there is between the magnanimity of a triennial Parliament, and that jealous haughtiness of prelates and cabin Counsellors that usurped of late, whenas they shall observe you in the midst of your victories and successes more gently brooking written exceptions against a voted order than other courts, which had produced nothing worth memory but the weak ostentation of wealth, would have endured the least signified dislike at any sudden proclamation.

If I should thus far presume upon the meek demeanor of your civil and gentle greatness, Lords and Commons, as what your published order has directly said, that to gainsay, I might defend myself with ease, if any should accuse me of being new or insolent, did they but know how much better I find you esteem it to imitate the old and elegant humanity of Greece, than the barbaric pride of a Hunnish and Norwegian stateliness. And out of those ages, to whose polite wisdom and letters we owe that we are not yet Goths and Jutlanders, I could name him [Isocrates] who from his private house wrote that discourse to the Parliament of Athens, that persuaded them to change the form of democracy which was then established. Such honor was done in those days to persons who professed the study of wisdom and eloquence, not only in their own country but in other lands, that cities and seignories heard them gladly and with great respect, if they had anything in public to admonish the state. Thus did Dion Prusaeus [Chrysostomos], a stranger and a private orator, counsel the Rhodians against a former edict; and I abound with other like examples, which to set here would be superfluous. But if from the industry of a life wholly dedicated to studious labors, and those natural endowments haply not the worst for two and fifty degrees of northern latitude, so much must be derogated, as to count me not equal to any of those who had this privilege, I would obtain to be thought not so inferior as yourselves are superior to the most of them who received their counsel: and how far you excel them, be assured, Lords and Commons, there can no greater testimony appear, than when your prudent spirit acknowledges and obeys the voice of reason from what quarter soever it be heard speaking, and renders you as willing to repeal any Act of your own setting forth, as any set forth by your predecessors.

If you be thus resolved, as it were injury to think you were not, I know not what should withhold me from presenting you with a fit instance wherein to show both that love of truth which you eminently profess, and that uprightness of your judgment which is not habitual to be partial to yourselves; by judging over again that Order which you have ordained *to regulate printing: That no book, pamphlet, or paper shall be henceforth printed, unless the same be first approved and licensed by such,* or at least one of such as shall be thereto appointed. For that part which preserves justly everyone's copy[right] to himself, or provides for the poor, I touch not, only wish they be not made pretenses to abuse and persecute honest and painful people, who offend not in either of these particulars. But that other clause of licensing books, which we thought had died with his brother *quadragesimal* and *matrimonial* when the prelates expired, I shall now attend with such a homily as shall lay before you, first, the inventors of it to be those whom you will be loath to own; next, what is to be thought in general of reading, whatever sort the books be; and that this Order avails nothing to the suppressing of scandalous, seditious, and libellous books, which were mainly intended to be suppressed. Last, that it will be primely to the discouragement of all learning, and the stop of truth, not only by disexercising and blunting our abilities in what we know already, but by hindering and cropping the discovery that might be yet further made both in religious and civil wisdom.

I deny not but that it is of greatest concernment in the Church and Commonwealth to have a vigilant eye how books demean themselves as well as persons; and thereafter to confine, imprison, and do sharpest justice on them as malefactors. For books are not absolutely dead things, but do contain a potency of life in them to be as active as that soul was whose progeny they are; nay, they do preserve as in a vial the purest efficacy and extraction of that living intellect that bred them. I know they are as lively, and as vigorously productive, as those fabulous dragon's teeth; and being sown up and down, may chance to spring up armed humans. And yet, on the other hand, unless wariness be used, as good almost kill a person as kill a good book: who kills a person kills a reasonable creature, God's image; but hu who destroys a good book, kills reason itself, kills the image of God, as it were, in the eye. Many a person lives a burden to the earth; but a good book is the precious life-blood of a master-spirit, embalmed and treasured up on purpose to a life beyond life. 'Tis true, no age can restore a life, whereof perhaps there is no great loss; and revolutions of ages do not often recover the loss of a rejected truth, for the lack of which whole nations fare the worse. We should be wary, therefore, what persecution we raise against the living labors of public persons, how we spill that seasoned life of humanity, preserved and stored up in books; since we see a kind of homicide may be thus committed, sometimes a martyrdom; and if it extend to the whole impression, a kind of massacre, whereof the execution ends not in the slaying of an elemental life, but strikes at that ethereal and fifth essence [quintessence], the breath of reason itself, slays an immortality rather than a life. But lest I should be condemned of introducing license, while I oppose licensing, I refuse not the pains to be so much historical as will serve to show what has been done by ancient and famous commonwealths against this disorder, till the very time that this project of licensing crept out of the Inquisition, was catched up by our prelates, and has caught some of our presbyters.

In Athens, where books and wits were ever busier than in any other part of Greece, I find but only two sorts of writings which the magistrates cared to take notice of; those either blasphemous and atheistical, or libellous. Thus the books of Protagoras were by the judges of Areopagus commanded to be burnt, and himself banished the territory for a discourse begun with his confessing not to know *whether there were gods, or whether not.* And against defaming, it was decreed that none should be traduced by name, as was the manner of *vetus comoedia*, whereby we may guess how they censured libelling; and this course was quick enough, as Cicero writes, to quell both the desperate wits of other atheists, and the open way of defaming, as the event showed. Of other sects and opinions, though tending to voluptuousness, and the denying of divine providence, they took no heed. Therefore we do not read that either Epicurus, or that libertine school of Cyrene, or what the Cynic impudence uttered, was ever questioned by the laws. Neither is it recorded that the writings of those old comedians were suppressed, though the acting of them were forbid; and that Plato commended the reading of Aristophanes, the loosest of them all, to his royal scholar

Dionysius, is commonly known, and may be excused, if holy [John] Chrysostom as is reported, nightly studied so much the same author, and had the art to cleanse a scurrilous vehemence into the style of a rousing sermon.

That other leading city of Greece, Lacedaemon, considering that Lycurgus their lawgiver was so addicted to elegant learning as to have been the first that brought out of Ionia the scattered works of Homer, and sent the poet Thales from Crete to prepare and mollify the Spartan surliness with his smooth songs and odes, the better to plant among them law and civility, it is to be wondered how museless and unbookish they were, minding nothing but the feats of war. There needed no licensing of books among them, for they disliked all but their own laconic apothegms, and took a slight occasion to chase Archilochus out of their city, perhaps for composing in a higher strain than their own soldierly ballads and roundels could reach to; or if it were for his broad verses, they were not therein so cautious, but they were as dissolute in their promiscuous conversing; whence Euripides affirms in *Andromache*, that their women were all unchaste. Thus much may give us light after what sort of books were prohibited among the Greeks.

The Romans also, for many ages trained up only to a military roughness, resembling most the Lacedaemonian guise, knew of learning little but what their Twelve Tables, and the Pontific College with their augurs and flamens taught them in religion and law, so unacquainted with other learning, that when Carneades and Critolaus, with the Stoic Diogenes coming ambassadors to Rome, took thereby occasion to give the city a taste of their philosophy, they were suspected for seducers by no less a person than Cato the Censor, who moved it in the Senate to dismiss them speedily, and to banish all such Attic babblers out of Italy. But Scipio and others of the noblest senators withstood him and his old Sabine austerity; honored and admired the men; and the Censor himself at last, in his old age, fell to the study of that whereof before he was so scrupulous. And yet at the same time, Naevius and Plautus, the first Latin comedians, had filled the city with all the borrowed scenes of Menander and Philemon.

Then began to be considered there also what was to be done to libellous books and authors; for Naevius was quickly cast into prison for his unbridled pen, and released by the tribunes upon his recantation; we read also that libels were burnt, and the makers punished by Augustus. The like severity, no doubt, was used, if anything were impiously written against their esteemed gods. Except in these two points, how the world went in books, the magistrate kept no reckoning. And therefore Lucretius without impeachment versifies his Epicurism to

Memmius, and had the honor to be set forth the second time by Cicero, so great a father of the commonwealth; although himself disputes against that opinion in his own writings. Nor was the satirical sharpness or naked plainness of Lucilius, or Catullus, or Flaccus [Quintus Horatius Flaccus, Horace] by any order prohibited.

And for matters of state, the story of Titus Livius [Livy], though it extolled that part which Pompey held, was not therefore suppressed by Octavius Caesar of the other faction. But that Naso [Publius Ovidius Naso, Ovid] was by him banished in his old age for the wanton poems of his youth, was but a mere covert of state over some secret cause: and besides, the books were neither banished nor called in. From hence we shall meet with little else but tyranny in the Roman Empire, that we may not marvel, if not so often bad as good books were silenced. I shall therefore deem to have been large enough in producing what among the ancients was punishable to write, save only which, all other arguments were free to treat on.

By this time the emperors were become Christians, whose discipline in this point I do not find to have been more severe than what was formerly in practice. The books of those whom they took to be grand heretics were examined, refuted, and condemned in the general councils; and not till then were prohibited, or burnt, by authority of the emperor. As for the writings of heathen authors, unless they were plain invectives against Christianity, as those of Porphyrius and Proclus, they met with no interdict that can be cited, till about the year 400, in a Carthaginian Council, wherein bishops themselves were forbid to read the books of Gentiles, but heresies they might read: while others long before them, on the contrary, scrupled more the books of heretics than of Gentiles. And that the primitive councils and bishops were inclined only to declare what books were not commendable, passing no further, but leaving it to each one's conscience to read or to lay by, till after the year 800, is observed already by Padre Paolo [Pietro Sarpi], the great unmasker of the Trentine Council.

After which time the Popes of Rome, engrossing what they pleased of political rule into their own hands, extended their dominion over people's eyes, as they had before over their judgments, burning and prohibiting to be read what they fancied not; yet sparing in their censures, and the books not many which they so dealt with; till Martin V, by his Bull, not only prohibited, but was the first that excommunicated the reading of heretical books; for about that time Wyclif and Huss growing terrible, were they who first drove the Papal Court to a stricter policy of prohibiting. Which course Leo X and his successors followed, until the Council of Trent and the Spanish Inquisition, engendering together, brought forth, or perfected those catalogues, and expurging indexes, that rake through the entrails of many an old good author, with a violation worse than any could be offered to hus tomb.

Nor did they stay in matters heretical, but any subject that was not to their palate, they either condemned in a prohibition, or had it straight into the new purgatory of an Index. To fill up the measure of encroachment, their last invention was to ordain that no book, pamphlet, or paper should be printed (as if St. Peter had bequeathed them the keys of the press also out of Paradise) unless it were approved and licensed under the hands of two or three glutton friars. For example:

Let the Chancellor Cini be pleased to see if in this present work be contained anything that may withstand the printing.

Vincent Rabbatta, Vicar of Florence.

I have seen this present work, and find nothing athwart the Catholic faith and good manners: in witness whereof I have given, &c.
Nicolò Cini, Chancellor of Florence.

Attending the precedent relation, it is allowed that this present work of Davanzati may be printed.

Vincent Rabbatta, Vicar of Florence.

It may be Printed, July 15.

Friar Simon Mompei d'Amelia,
Chancellor of the holy office in Florence.

Sure they have a conceit, if he of the bottomless pit had not long since broke prison, that this quadruple exorcism would bar him down. I fear their next design will be to get into their custody the licensing of that which they say Claudius intended, but went not through with [*Quo veniem daret flatum crepitumque ventris in convivio emittendi—Suetonius*]. Vouchsafe to see another of their forms, the Roman stamp:

Imprimatur, If it seem good to the reverend Master of the Holy Palace,
Belcastro, Viceregent.

Imprimatur,

Friar Nicolò Rodolphi, Master of the Holy Palace.

Sometimes five *Imprimaturs* [Latin for "It may be printed"] are seen together, dialoguewise, in the piazza of one title-page, complimenting and ducking each to other with their shaven reverences, whether the author, who stands by in perplexity at the foot of hus epistle, shall to the press or to the sponge. These are the pretty responsories, these are the dear antiphonies that so bewitched of late our prelates and their chaplains with the goodly echo they made; and besotted us to the gay imitation of a lordly *Imprimatur*, one from Lambeth House [residence of the Archbishop of Canterbury], another from the west end of [St.] Paul's [headquarters of the Bishop of London], so apishly romanizing that the word of command still was set down in Latin; as if the learned grammatical pen that wrote it would cast no ink without Latin; or perhaps, as they thought, because no vulgar tongue was worthy to express the pure conceit of an *Imprimatur*; but rather, as I hope, for that our English, the language of people ever famous and foremost in the achievements of liberty, will not easily find servile letters enough to spell such a dictatory presumption English.

And thus you have the inventors and the original of book-licensing ripped up and drawn as lineally as any pedigree. We have it not, that can be heard of, from any ancient state, or polity, or church, nor by any statute left us by our ancestors elder or later; nor from the modern custom of any reformed city or church abroad; but from the most anti-christian council and the most tyrannous inquisition that ever inquired.

Till then books were ever as freely admitted into the world as any other birth; the issue of the brain was no more stifled than the issue of the womb; no envious Juno sat cross-legged over the nativity of anyone's intellectual offspring; but if it proved a monster, who denies but that it was justly burnt, or sunk into the sea. But that a book, in worse condition than a peccant soul, should be to stand before a jury before it be born to the world, and undergo yet in darkness the judgment of Radamanth and his colleagues, before it can pass the ferry backward into light, was never heard before, till that mysterious iniquity, provoked and troubled at the first entrance of Reformation, sought out new limbos and new hells wherein they might include our books also within the number of their damned. And this was the rare morsel so officiously snatched up, and so ill-favoredly imitated by our inquisiturient bishops, and the attendant minorites, their chaplains. That you like not now these most certain authors of this licensing order, and that all sinister intention was far distant from your thoughts, when you were importuned the passing it, all people know the integrity of your actions, and how you honor truth, will clear you readily.

But some will say, what though the inventors were bad, the thing for all that may be good. It may so; yet if that thing be no such deep invention, but obvious and easy for anyone to light on, and yet best and wisest commonwealths through all ages and occasions have forborne to use it, and falsest seducers and oppressors of humans were the first who took it up, and to no other purpose but to obstruct and hinder the first approach of Reformation; I am of those who believe it will be a harder alchemy than Lullius [Raymond Lully] ever knew to sublimate any good use out of such an invention. Yet this only is what I request to gain from this reason, that it may be held a dangerous and suspicious fruit, as certainly it deserves, for the tree that bore it, until I can dissect one by one the properties it has. But I have first to finish, as was propounded, what is to be thought in general of reading books, whatever sort they be, and whether be more the benefit or the harm that thence proceeds?

Not to insist upon the examples of Moses, Daniel, and Paul, who were skilful in all the learning of the Egyptians, Chaldeans, and Greeks, which could not probably be without reading their books of all sorts; in Paul especially, who thought it no defilement to insert into holy Scripture the sentences of three Greek poets, and one of them a tragedian; the question was notwithstanding sometimes controverted among the primitive doctors, but with great odds on that side which affirmed it both lawful and profitable, as was then evidently perceived when Julian the Apostate and subtlest enemy to our faith, made a decree forbidding Christians the study of heathen learning; for, said he, they wound us with our own weapons, and with our own arts and sciences they overcome us. And, indeed, the Christians were put so to their shifts by this crafty means, and so much in danger to decline into all ignorance, that the two Apollinarii were compelled, as a person may say, to coin all the seven liberal sciences out of the Bible, reducing it to diverse forms of orations, poems, dialogues, even to the calculating of a new Christian grammar. But, says the historian Socrates [Scholasticus], the providence of God provided better than the industry of Apollinarius and his son, by taking away that illiterate law with the life of him who devised it.

So great an injury they then held it to be deprived of Hellenic learning; and thought it a persecution more undermining, and secretly decaying the Church, than the open cruelty of Decius or Diocletian. And perhaps it was the same politic drift that the devil whipped St. Jerome in a Lenten dream for reading Cicero; or else it was a phantasm bred by the fever which had then seized him. For had an angel been his discipliner, unless it were for dwelling too much upon Ciceronianisms, and had chastised the reading, not the vanity, it had been plainly partial; first to correct him for grave Cicero, and not for scurril Plautus, whom he confesses to have been reading not long before; next to correct him only, and let so many more ancient Parents wax old in those pleasant and florid studies without the lash of such a tutoring apparition; insomuch that Basil teaches how some good use may be made of *Margites*, a sportful poem not now extant writ by Homer; and why not then of *Morgante*, an Italian romance much to the same purpose?

But if it be agreed we shall be tried by visions, there is a vision recorded by Eusebius, far ancienter than this tale of Jerome to the nun Eustochium, and, besides, has nothing of a fever in it. Dionysius Alexandrinus was, about the year 240, a person of great name in the Church for piety and learning, who customarily availed himself much against heretics by being conversant in their books; until a certain presbyter laid it scrupulously to his conscience, how he dared venture himself among those defiling volumes. The worthy man, loath to give offence, fell into a new debate with himself what was to be thought; when suddenly a vision sent from God (it is his own *Epistle* that so avers it) confirmed him in these words: "Read any books whatever come to your hands, for you are sufficient both to judge aright and to examine each matter." To this revelation he assented the sooner, as he confesses, because it was answerable to that of the Apostle to the Thessalonians: "Prove all things, hold fast that which is good."

And he might have added another remarkable saying of the same author: "To the pure, all things are pure"; not only meats and drinks, but all kind of knowledge whether of good or evil; the knowledge cannot defile, nor consequently the books, if the will and conscience be not defiled. For books are as meats and viands are—some of good, some of evil substance— and yet God in that unapocryphal vision said without exception, "Rise, Peter, kill and eat," leaving the choice to each person's discretion. Wholesome meats to a vitiated stomach differ little or nothing from unwholesome, and best books to a naughty mind are not unappliable to occasions of evil. Bad meats will scarce breed good nourishment in the healthiest concoction; but herein the difference is of bad books, that they to a discreet and judicious reader serve in many respects to discover, to confute, to forewarn, and to illustrate.

Whereof what better witness can you expect I should produce than one of your own now sitting in Parliament, the chief of learned men reputed in this land, Mr. Selden; whose volume of natural and national laws proves, not only by great authorities brought together, but by exquisite reasons and theorems almost mathematically demonstrative, that all opinions, yea errors, known, read, and collated, are of main service and assistance toward the speedy attainment of what is truest.

I conceive, therefore, that when God did enlarge the universal diet of the human body, saving ever the rules of temperance, hu then also, as before, left arbitrary the dieting and repasting of our minds; as wherein every mature person might have to exercise hus own leading capacity. How great a virtue is temperance, how much of moment through the whole life of humanity! Yet God commits the managing so great a trust, without particular law or prescription, wholly to the demeanor of every grown person. And therefore, when hu humself tabled the Jews from heaven, that omer, which was everyone's daily portion of manna, is computed to have been more than might have well sufficed the heartiest feeder thrice as many meals. For those actions which enter into a person, rather than issue out of hum, and therefore defile not, God uses not to captivate under a perpetual childhood of prescription, but trusts hum with the gift of reason to be hus own chooser; there were but little work left for preaching, if law and compulsion should grow so fast upon those things which heretofore were governed only by exhortation. Solomon informs us that much reading is a weariness to the flesh; but neither he nor other inspired author tells us that such or such reading is unlawful; yet certainly had God thought good to limit us herein, it had been much more expedient to have told us what was unlawful, than what was wearisome.

As for the burning of those Ephesian books by St. Paul's converts; 'tis replied the books were magic, the Syriac so renders them. It was a private act, a voluntary act, and leaves us to a voluntary imitation: the persons in remorse burnt those books which were their own; the magistrate by this example is not appointed; these people practised the books, another might perhaps have read them in some sort usefully.

Good and evil we know in the field of this world grow up together almost inseparably; and the knowledge of good is so involved and interwoven with the knowledge of evil, and in so many cunning resemblances hardly to be discerned, that those confused seeds which were imposed upon Psyche as an incessant labor to cull out, and sort asunder, were not more intermixed. It was from out the rind of one apple tasted, that the knowledge of good and evil, as two twins cleaving together, leaped forth into the world. And perhaps this is that doom which Adam fell into of knowing good and evil, that is to say, of knowing good by evil.

As therefore the state of humanity now is, what wisdom can there be to choose, what continence to forbear without the knowledge of evil? Hu that can apprehend and consider vice with all hus baits and seeming pleasures, and yet abstain, and yet distinguish, and yet prefer that which is truly better, hu is the true wayfaring Christian. I cannot praise a fugitive and cloistered virtue, unexercised and unbreathed, that never sallies out and sees hus adversary, but slinks out of the race where that immortal garland is to be run for, not without dust and heat.

Assuredly we bring not innocence into the world, we bring impurity much rather: that which purifies us is trial, and trial is by what is contrary. That virtue therefore which is but a youngling in the contemplation of evil, and knows not the utmost that vice promises to hus followers, and rejects it, is but a blank virtue, not a pure; hus whiteness is but an excremental whiteness; which was the reason why our sage and serious poet Spenser, whom I dare be known to think a better teacher than Scotus or Aquinas, describing true temperance under the person of Guyon, brings him in with his palmer through the cave of Mammon and the bower of earthly bliss, that he might see and know, and yet abstain.

Since therefore, the knowledge and survey of vice is in this world so necessary to the constituting of human virtue, and the scanning of error to the confirmation of truth, how can we more safely, and with less danger, scout into the regions of sin and falsity, than by reading all manner of tractates and hearing all manner of reason? And this is the benefit which may be had of books promiscuously read.

But of the harm that may result hence, three kinds are usually reckoned. First is feared the infection that may spread; but then all human learning and controversy in religious points must remove out of the world, even the Bible itself; for that often relates blasphemy not nicely, it describes the carnal sense of wicked people not inelegantly, it brings in holiest persons passionately murmuring against providence through all the arguments of Epicurus; in other great disputes it answers dubiously and darkly to the common reader. And ask a Talmudist what ails the modesty of hus marginal *Keri* [text as spoken], that Moses and all the prophets cannot persuade hum to pronounce the textual *Chetiv* [written text]. For these causes we all know the Bible itself put by the Papist into the first rank of prohibited books. The most ancient Parents must be next removed, as Clement of Alexandria, and that Eusebian book of Evangelic preparation transmitting our ears through a hoard of heathenish obscenities to receive the Gospel. Who finds not that Irenaeus, Epiphanius, Jerome, and others discover more heresies than they well confute, and that often for heresy which is the truer opinion?

Nor does it help to say for these and all the heathen writers of greatest infection, if it must be thought so, with whom is bound up the life of human learning, that they writ in an unknown tongue, so long as we are sure those languages are known as well to the worst of persons, who are both most able and most diligent to instil the poison they suck, first into the courts of princes, acquainting them with the choicest delights, and criticisms of sin. As perhaps did that Petronius whom Nero called his Arbiter, the master of his revels; and that notorious ribald of Arezzo (Pietro Aretino), dreaded and yet dear to the Italian courtiers. I name not him for posterity's sake, whom Harry VIII named in merriment his Vicar of Hell. By which compendious way all the contagion that foreign books can infuse, will find a passage to the people far easier and shorter than an Indian voyage, though it could be sailed either by the north of Cathay eastward, or of Canada westward, while our Spanish licensing gags the English press never so severely.

But, on the other side, that infection which is from books of controversy in religion, is more doubtful and dangerous to the learned than to the ignorant; and yet those books must be permitted untouched by the licenser. It will be hard to instance where any ignorant human has been ever seduced by papistical book in English, unless it were commended and expounded to hum by some of that clergy; and indeed all such tractates, whether false or true, are as the prophecy of Isaiah was to the eunuch, "not to be understood without a guide." But of our priests and doctors how many have been corrupted by studying the comments of Jesuits and Sorbonists, and how fast they could transfuse that corruption into the people, our experience is both late and sad. It is not forgot, since the acute and distinct Arminius was perverted merely by the perusing of a nameless discourse written at Delft, which at first he took in hand to confute.

Seeing, therefore, that those books, and those in great abundance, which are most likely to taint both life and doctrine, cannot be suppressed without the fall of learning, and of all ability in disputation; and that these books of either sort are most and soonest catching to the learned, from whom to the common people whatever is heretical or dissolute may quickly be conveyed; and that evil manners are as perfectly learned without books a thousand other ways which cannot be stopped; and evil doctrine not with books can propagate, except a teacher guide, which hu might also do without writing, and so beyond prohibiting: I am not able to unfold how this cautelous enterprise of licensing can be exempted from the number of vain and impossible attempts. And hu who were pleasantly disposed, could not well avoid to liken it to the exploit of that gallant person who thought to pound up the crows by shutting hus park gate.

Besides another inconvenience, if learned persons be the first receivers out of books and dispreaders both of vice and error, how shall the licensers themselves be confided in, unless we can confer upon them, or they assume to themselves above all others in the land, the grace of infallibility and uncorruptedness? And again, if it be true that a wise

21

person, like a good refiner, can gather gold out of the drossiest volume, and that a fool will be a fool with the best book, yes or without book, there is no reason that we should deprive a wise person of any advantage to hus wisdom, while we seek to restrain from a fool that which being restrained will be no hindrance to hus folly. For if there should be so much exactness always used to keep that from hum which is unfit for hus reading, we should, in the judgment of Aristotle, not only, but of Solomon and of our Saviour, not vouchsafe hum good precepts, and by consequence not willingly admit hum to good books; as being certain that a wise person will make better use of an idle pamphlet than a fool will do of sacred Scripture.

'Tis next alleged we must not expose ourselves to temptations without necessity, and, next to that, not employ our time in vain things. To both these objections one answer will serve, out of the grounds already laid; that to all people such books are not temptations nor vanities, but useful drugs and materials wherewith to temper and compose effective and strong medicines which human life cannot lack. The rest, as children and childish humans, who have not the art to qualify and prepare these working minerals, well may be exhorted to forbear, but hindered forcibly they cannot be by all the licensing that sainted Inquisition could ever yet contrive. Which is what I promised to deliver next: that this order of licensing conduces nothing to the end for which it was framed; and has almost prevented me by being clear already, while thus much has been explaining. See the ingenuity of Truth, who, when hu gets a free and willing hand, opens humself faster than the pace of method and discourse can overtake hum.

It was the task which I began with, to show that no nation, or well instituted state, if they valued books at all, did ever use this way of licensing; and it might be answered, that this is a piece of prudence lately discovered. To which I return, that as it was a thing slight and obvious to think on, so if it had been difficult to find out, there did not lack among them long since who suggested such a course; which they not following, leave us a pattern of their judgment that it was not the not knowing, but the not approving, which was the cause of their not using it.

Plato, a man of high authority indeed, but least of all for his commonwealth, in the book of his *Laws*, which no city ever yet received, fed his fancy with making many edicts to his airy burgomasters, which they who otherwise admire him, wish had been rather buried and excused in the genial cups of an Academic night-sitting. By which laws he seems to tolerate no kind of learning, but by unalterable decree, consisting most of practical traditions, to the attainment whereof a library of smaller bulk than his own *Dialogues* would be abundant. And there also enacts that no poet should so much as read to any private person what hu had written, until the judges and lawkeepers had seen it and allowed it; but that Plato meant this law peculiarly to that commonwealth which he had imagined, and to no other, is evident. Why was he not else a lawgiver himself, but a transgressor, and to be expelled by his own magistrates; both for the wanton epigrams and dialogues which he made, and his perpetual reading of Sophron, Mimus, and Aristophanes, books of grossest infamy; and also for commending the latter of them, though he were the malicious libeller of his chief friends, to be read by the tyrant Dionysius, who had little need of such trash to spend his time on? But that he knew this licensing of poems had reference and dependence to many other provisos there set down in his fancied Republic, which in this world could have no place; and so neither he himself, nor any magistrate, or city ever imitated that course, which, taken apart from those other collateral injunctions, must certainly be vain and fruitless.

For if they fell upon one kind of strictness, unless their care were equal to regulate all other things of like aptness to corrupt the mind, that single endeavor they knew would be but a fond labor; to shut and fortify one gate against corruption, and be necessitated to leave others round about wide open. If we think to regulate printing, thereby to rectify manners, we must regulate all recreations and pastimes, all that is delightful to people. No music must be heard, no song be set or sung, but what is grave and Doric. There must be licensing dancers, that no gesture, motion, or deportment be taught our youth, but what by their allowance shall be thought honest; for such Plato was provided of. It will ask more than the work of twenty licensers to examine all the lutes, the violins, and the guitars in every house; they must not be suffered to prattle as they do, but must be licensed what they may say. And who shall silence all the airs and madrigals that whisper softness in chambers? The windows also, and the balconies must be thought on; there are shrewd books, with dangerous frontispieces, set to sale; who shall prohibit them? Shall twenty licensers? The villages also must have their visitors to inquire what lectures the bagpipe and the rebeck reads even to the balladry, and the gamut of every municipal fiddler, for these are the countryperson's Arcadias, and hus Monte Mayors.

Next, what more national corruption, for which England hears ill abroad, than household gluttony? Who shall be the rectors of our daily rioting? And what shall be done to inhibit the multitudes that frequent those houses where drunkenness is sold and harbored? Our garments also should be referred to the licensing of some more sober workmasters,

23

dissemination

private → public

Marshall McLuhan.
'Understanding Media'

to see them cut into a less wanton garb. Who shall regulate all the mixed conversation of our youth, male and female together, as is the fashion of this country? Who shall still appoint what shall be discoursed, what presumed, and no further? Lastly, who shall forbid and separate all idle resort, all evil company? These things will be, and must be; but how they shall be least hurtful, how least enticing, herein consists the grave and governing wisdom of a state.

To sequester out of the world into Atlantic and Utopian polities, which never can be drawn into use, will not mend our condition; but to ordain wisely as in this world of evil, in the midst whereof God has placed us unavoidably. Nor is it Plato's licensing of books will do this, which necessarily pulls along with it so many other kinds of licensing as will make us all both ridiculous and weary, and yet frustrate; but those unwritten, or at least unconstraining, laws of virtuous education, religious and civil nurture, which Plato there mentions as the bonds and ligaments of the commonwealth, the pillars and the sustainers of every written statute; these they be which will bear chief sway in such matters as these, when all licensing will be easily eluded. Impunity and remissness, for certain, are the bane of a commonwealth; but here the great art lies, to discern in what the law is to bid restraint and punishment, and in what things persuasion only is to work. If every action which is good or evil in humans at ripe years, were to be under pittance and prescription and compulsion, what were virtue but a name, what praise could be then due to well-doing, what gramercy to be sober, just, or continent?

Many there be that complain of divine Providence for suffering Adam to transgress. Foolish tongues! when God gave him reason, hu gave him freedom to choose, for reason is but choosing; he had been else a mere artificial Adam, such an Adam as he is in the motions (puppet shows). We ourselves esteem not of that obedience, or love, or gift, which is of force. God, therefore, left him free, set before him a provoking object, ever almost in his eyes; herein consisted his merit, herein the right of his reward, the praise of his abstinence. Wherefore did hu create passions within us, pleasures round about us, but that these rightly tempered are the very ingredients of virtue? They are not skilful considerers of human things, who imagine to remove sin by removing the matter of sin. For, besides that it is a huge heap increasing under the very act of diminishing, though some part of it may for a time be withdrawn from some persons, it cannot from all, in such a universal thing as books are; and when this is done, yet the sin remains entire. Though you take from a covetous human all hus treasure, hu has yet one jewel left—you cannot bereave hum of hus covetousness. Banish all objects of lust, shut up all youth into the severest discipline that can be exercised in any hermitage, you cannot make them chaste, that came not there so: such great care and wisdom is required to the right managing of this point.

Suppose we could expel sin by this means; look how much we thus expel of sin, so much we expel of virtue: for the matter of them both is the same; remove that, and you remove them both alike. This justifies the high providence of God, who, though hu command us temperance, justice, continence, yet pours out before us, even to a profuseness, all desirable things, and gives us minds that can wander beyond all limit and satiety. Why should we then affect a rigor contrary to the manner of God and of nature, by abridging or scanting those means which books freely permitted are, both to the trial of virtue, and the exercise of truth?

It would be better done to learn that the law must surely be frivolous which goes to restrain things uncertainly and yet equally working to good and to evil. And were I the chooser, a dram of well-doing should be preferred before many times as much the forcible hindrance of evil-doing. For God sure esteems the growth and completing of one virtuous person more than the restraint of ten vicious. And though whatever thing we hear or see, sitting, walking, travelling, or conversing, may be fitly called our book, and is of the same effect that writings are; yet grant the thing to be prohibited were only books, it appears that this order up to the present is far insufficient to the end which it intends. Do we not see—not once or oftener, but weekly—that continued court-libel (*Mercurius Aulicus, Court Mercury* published by King Charles from Oxford) against the Parliament and City printed, as the wet sheets can witness, and dispersed among us, for all that licensing can do? Yet this is the prime service a person would think, wherein this Order should give proof of itself. If it were executed, you'll say. But certain, if execution be remiss or blindfold now, and in this particular, what will it be hereafter and in other books?

If then the Order shall not be vain and frustrate, behold a new labor, Lords and Commons. You must repeal and proscribe all scandalous and unlicensed books already printed and divulged (after you have drawn them up into a list, that all may know which are condemned and which not) and ordain that no foreign books be delivered out of custody till they have been read over. This office will require the whole time of not a few overseers, and those no vulgar persons. There be also books which are partly useful and excellent, partly culpable and pernicious; this work will ask as many more officials to make expurgations and expunctions, that the commonwealth of learning be not damnified. In short, when the multitude of books increase upon their hands, you must be ready to catalogue all those printers who are found frequently offending, and forbid the importation of their whole suspected typography. In a word, that this your Order may be exact and not deficient, you must reform it perfectly according to the model of Trent and Seville, which I know you abhor to do.

Yet, though you should condescend to this, which God forbid, the Order still would be but fruitless and defective to that end whereto you meant it. If to prevent sects and schisms, who is so unread or so uncatechized in story that has not heard of many sects refusing books as a hindrance, and preserving their doctrine unmixed for many ages, only by unwritten traditions? The Christian faith, for that was once a schism, is not unknown to have spread all over Asia, before any Gospel or Epistle was seen in writing. If the amendment of manners be aimed at, look into Italy and Spain, whether those places be one scruple the better, the honester, the wiser, the chaster, since all the inquisitional rigor that has been executed upon books.

Another reason whereby to make it plain that this Order will miss the end it seeks, consider by the quality which ought to be in every licenser. It cannot be denied but that hu who is made judge to sit upon the birth or death of books, whether they may be wafted into the world or not, had need to be a person above the common measure, both studious, learned, and judicious. There may be else no mean mistakes in the censure of what is passable or not, which is also no mean injury. If hu be of such worth as is required, there cannot be a more tedious and unpleasing journey-work, a greater loss of time levied upon hus head, than to be made the perpetual reader of unchosen books and pamphlets, ofttimes huge volumes. There is no book that is acceptable unless at certain seasons; but to be enjoined the reading of that at all times, and in a hand scarce legible, whereof three pages would not down at any time in the fairest print, is an imposition which I cannot believe how hu that values time and hus own studies, or is but of a sensible nostril, should be able to endure.

In this one thing I crave leave of the present licensers to be pardoned for so thinking; who doubtless took this office up, looking on it through their obedience to the Parliament, whose command perhaps made all things seem easy and unlaborious to them; but that this short trial has wearied them out already, their own expressions and excuses to them who make so many journeys to solicit their license, are testimony enough. Seeing, therefore, those who now possess the employment, by all evident signs wish themselves well rid of it, and that no person of worth, none that is not a plain unthrift of hus own hours, is ever likely to succeed them, except hu mean to put humself to the salary of a press corrector, we may easily foresee what kind of licensers we are to expect hereafter, either ignorant, imperious, and remiss, or basely pecuniary. This is what I had to show, wherein this Order cannot conduce to that end whereof it bears the intention.

I lastly proceed from the no good it can do, to the manifest hurt it causes in being, first, the greatest discouragement and affront that can be offered to learning and to learned persons. It was the complaint and lamentation of prelates, upon every least breath of a motion to remove pluralities and distribute more equally church revenues, that then all learning would be forever dashed and discouraged. But as for that opinion, I never found cause to think that the tenth part of learning stood or fell with the clergy; nor could I ever but hold it for a sordid and unworthy speech of any churchperson who had a competency left hum. If, therefore, you be loath to dishearten utterly and discontent, not the mercenary crew of false pretenders to learning, but the free and ingenuous sort of such as evidently were born to study and love learning for itself, not for lucre, or any other end but the service of God and of truth, and perhaps that lasting fame and perpetuity of praise which God and good people have consented shall be the reward of those whose published labors advance the good of humanity; then know, that so far to distrust the judgment and the honesty of one who has but a common repute in learning, and never yet offended, as not to count hum fit to print hus mind without a tutor and examiner, lest hu should drop a schism, or something of corruption, is the greatest displeasure and indignity to a free and knowing spirit that can be put upon hum.

What advantage is it to be an adult over it is to be a boy or girl at school, if we have only escaped the ferula to come under the fescue of an *Imprimatur*; if serious and elaborate writings, as if they were no more than the theme of a grammar-kid under hus pedagogue, must not be uttered without the cursory eyes of a temporizing and extemporizing licenser? Hu who is not trusted with hus own actions, hus drift not being known to be evil, and standing to the hazard of law and penalty, has no great argument to think humself reputed in the commonwealth wherein hu was born for other than a fool or a foreigner.

When a person writes to the world, hu summons up all hus reason and deliberation to assist hum; hu searches, meditates, is industrious, and likely consults and confers with hus judicious friends, after all which done hu takes humself to be informed in what hu writes, as well as any that wrote before hum. If in this the most consummate act of hus fidelity and ripeness, no years, no industry, no former proof of hus abilities can bring hum to that state of maturity as not to be still mistrusted and suspected unless hu carry all hus considerate diligence, all hus midnight watchings, and expense of Palladian oil, to the hasty view of an unleisured licenser, perhaps much hus younger, perhaps far hus inferior in judgment, perhaps one who never knew the labor of book-writing, and if hu be not repulsed or slighted, must appear in print like a puny with hus guardian and hus censor's hand on the back of hus title to be hus bail and surety that hu is no idiot or seducer; it cannot be but a dishonor and derogation to the author, to the book, to the privilege and dignity of learning.

And what if the author shall be one so copious of fancy as to have many things well worth the adding, come into hus mind after licensing, while the book is yet under the press, which not seldom happens to the best and most diligent writers; and that perhaps a dozen times in one book. The printer dares not go beyond hus licensed copy. So often then must the author trudge to hus leave-giver, that those hus new insertions may be viewed, and many a jaunt will be made, before that licenser, for it must be the same person, can either be found, or found at leisure. Meanwhile, either the press must stand still, which is no small damage, or the author lose his most accurate thoughts, and send the book forth worse than hu had made it, which to a diligent writer is the greatest melancholy and vexation that can befall.

And how can a person teach with authority, which is the life of teaching, how can hu be a doctor in hus book as hu ought to be, or else had better be silent, whenas all hu teaches, all hu delivers, is but under the tuition, of the correction of hus partriarchal licenser to blot or alter what precisely accords not with the hide-bound humor which hu calls hus judgment? When every acute reader upon the first sight of a pedantic license, will be ready with these like words to ding the book a quoit's distance from him: "I hate a pupil teacher, I endure not an instructor that comes to me under the wardship of an overseeing fist. I know nothing of the licenser, but that I have hus own hand here for hus arrogance; who shall warrant me hus judgment?"

"The State, sir," replies the stationer, but has a quick return: "The State shall be my governors, but not my critics; they may be mistaken in the choice of a licenser, as easily as this licenser may be mistaken in an author; this is some common stuff"; and hu might add from Sir Francis Bacon, that "Such authorized books are but the language of the times." For though a licenser should happen to be judicious more than ordinary, which will be a great jeopardy of the next succession, yet hus very office, and hus commission enjoins hum to let pass nothing but what is vulgarly received already.

No, which is more lamentable, if the work of any deceased author, though never so famous in hus lifetime, and even to this day, come to their hands for license to be printed, or reprinted; if there be found in hus book one sentence of a venturous edge, uttered in the height of zeal, and who knows whether it might not be the dictate of a divine spirit, yet not suiting with every low, decrepit humor of their own, though it were Knox himself, the reformer of a kingdom, that spoke it, they will not pardon him their dash; the sense of that great person shall to all posterity be lost, for the fearfulness, or the presumptuous rashness, of a perfunctory licenser. And to what an author this violence has been lately done, and in what book of greatest consequence to be faithfully published, I could now instance, but shall forbear till a more convenient season.

Yet if these things be not resented seriously and timely by them who have the remedy in their power, but that such iron-molds as these shall have authority to gnaw out the choicest periods of most exquisite books, and to commit such a treacherous fraud against the orphan remainders of worthiest humans after death, the more sorrow will belong to that hapless race of persons whose misfortune it is to have understanding. Henceforth, let no one care to learn, or care to be more than worldly wise; for certainly in higher matters to be ignorant and slothful, to be a common steadfast dunce, will be the only pleasant life, and only in request.

And as it is a particular disesteem of every knowing person alive, and most injurious to the written labors and monuments of the dead, so to me it seems an undervaluing and vilifying of the whole nation. I cannot set so light by all the invention, the art, the wit, the grave and solid judgment which is in England, as that it can be comprehended in any twenty capacities how good soever; much less that it should not pass except their superintendence be over it, except it be sifted and strained with their strainers; that it should be uncurrent without their manual stamp. Truth and understanding are not such wares as to be monopolized and traded in by tickets and statutes and standards. We must not think to make a staple commodity of all the knowledge in the land, to mark and license it like our broadcloth and our woolpacks. What is it but a servitude like that imposed by the Philistines, not to be allowed the sharpening of our own axes and coulters, but we must repair from all quarters to twenty licensing forges.

Had anyone written and divulged erroneous things and scandalous to honest life, misusing and forfeiting the esteem had of hus reason among people; if, after conviction, this only censure were adjudged hum, that hu should never henceforth write, but what were first examined by an appointed officer, whose hand should be annexed to pass hus credit for hum, that now hu might be safely read; it could not be apprehended less than a disgraceful punishment.

Therefore, to include the whole nation, and those that never yet thus offended, under such a diffident and suspectful prohibition, may plainly be understood what a disparagement it is. So much the more, when debtors and delinquents may walk abroad without a keeper, but unoffensive books must not stir forth without a visible jailor in their title. Nor is it to the common people less than a reproach; for if we be so jealous over them as that we dare not trust them with an English pamphlet, what do we but censure them for a giddy, vicious, and ungrounded people; in such a sick and weak state of faith and discretion, as to be able to take nothing down but through the pipe of a licenser? That this is care or love of them, we cannot pretend, when in those popish places where the laity are most hated and despised, the same strictness is used over them. Wisdom we cannot call it, because it stops but one breach of license, nor that neither; when those corruptions which it seeks to prevent, break in faster at other doors which cannot be shut.

And in conclusion, it reflects to the disrepute of our ministers also, of whose labors we should hope better, and of the proficiency which their flock reaps by them, than that after all this light of the Gospel which is and is to be, and all this continual preaching, they should be still frequented with such an unprincipled, unedified, and laic rabble, as that the whiff of every new pamphlet should stagger them out of their catechism and Christian walking. This may have much reason to discourage the ministers, when such a low conceit is had of all their exhortations and the benefiting of their hearers, as that they are not thought fit to be turned loose to three sheets of paper without a licenser; that all the sermons, all the lectures preached, printed, vented in such numbers, and such volumes, as have now well-nigh made all other books unsaleable, should not be armor enough against one single enchiridion, without the castle St. Angelo of an *Imprimatur*.

And lest some should persuade you, Lords and Commons, that these arguments of learned persons' discouragement at this your Order are mere flourishes, and not real, I could recount what I have seen and heard in other countries where this kind of inquisition tyrannizes; when I have sat among their learned ones, for that honor I had, and been counted happy to be born in such a place of philosophic freedom as they supposed England was, while themselves did nothing but bemoan the servile condition into which learning among them was brought; that this was it which had damped the glory of Italian wits; that nothing had been there written now these many years but flattery and fustian. There it was that I found and visited the famous Galileo, grown old, a prisoner to the Inquisition for thinking in astronomy otherwise than the Franciscan and Dominican licensers thought. And though I knew that

England then was groaning loudest under the prelatical yoke, nevertheless I took it as a pledge of future happiness that other nations were so persuaded of its liberty.

Yet was it beyond my hope that those worthies were then breathing in its air, who should be its leaders to such a deliverance as shall never be forgotten by any revolution of time that this world has to finish. When that was once begun, it was as little in my fear, that what words of complaint I heard among learned persons of other parts uttered against the Inquisition, the same I should hear by as learned persons at home uttered in time of Parliament against an Order of licensing; and that so generally, that when I had disclosed myself a companion of their discontent, I might say, if without envy, that he [Cicero] whom an honest quaestorship had endeared to the Sicilians, was not more by them importuned against Verres, than the favorable opinion which I had among many who honor you, and are known and respected by you, loaded me with entreaties and persuasions that I would not despair to lay together that which just reason should bring into my mind toward the removal of an undeserved slavery upon learning.

That this is not, therefore, the disburdening of a particular fancy, but the common grievance of all those who had prepared their minds and studies above the vulgar pitch to advance truth in others, and from others to entertain it, thus much may satisfy. And in their name I shall for neither friend nor foe conceal what the general murmur is; that if it come to inquisitioning again and licensing, and that we are so timorous of ourselves and so suspicious of everybody as to fear each book and the shaking of every leaf, before we know what the contents are; if some who but of late were little better than silenced from preaching, shall come now to silence us from reading, except what they please, it cannot be guessed what is intended by some but a second tyranny over learning; and will soon put it out of controversy that bishops and presbyters are the same to us both name and thing.

That those evils of prelaty which before from five or six and twenty sees were distributively charged upon the whole people, will now light wholly upon learning, is not obscure to us; since now the pastor of a small unlearned parish, on the sudden shall be exalted archbishop over a large diocese of books, and yet not remove, but keep hus other cure too, a mystical pluralist. Hu who but of late cried down the sole ordination of every novice bachelor of art, and denied sole jurisdiction over the simplest parishioner, shall now at home in hus private chair assume both these over worthiest and most excellent books and ablest authors that write them. This is not, you covenants and protestations that we have made, this is not to put down prelaty; this is but to chop an episcopacy; this is but to translate the palace metropolitan from one kind of dominion into another; this is but an old canonical sleight of commuting our penance. To startle thus quickly at a mere unlicensed pamphlet will after a while be afraid of every conventicle, and a while after will make a conventicle of every Christian meeting.

But I am certain that a state governed by the rules of justice and fortitude, or a church built and founded upon the rock of faith and true knowledge, cannot be so pusillanimous. While things are yet not constituted in religion, that freedom of writing should be restrained by a discipline imitated from the prelates, and learned by them from the Inquisition, to shut us up all again into the breast of a licenser, must give cause of doubt and discouragement to all learned and religious persons. Who cannot but discern the fineness of this politic drift, and who are the contrivers: that while bishops were to be baited down, then all presses might be open; it was the people's birthright and privilege in time of Parliament, it was the breaking forth of light.

But now, the bishops abrogated and voided out of the Church, as if our Reformation sought no more, but to make room for others into their seats under another name, the episcopal arts begin to bud again; the cruise of truth must run no more oil; liberty of printing must be enslaved again under a prelatical commission of twenty, the privilege of the people nullified; and, which is worse, the freedom of learning must groan again, and to its old fetters: all this the Parliament yet sitting. Although their own late arguments and defenses against the prelates might remember them that this obstructing violence meets for the most part with an event utterly opposite to the end which it drives at; instead of suppressing sects and schisms, it raises them and invests them with a reputation: "The punishing of wits enhances their authority," says the Viscount St. Albans, "and a forbidden writing is thought to be a certain spark of truth that flies up in the faces of them who seek to tread it out."

This Order, therefore, may prove a nursing mother to sects, but I shall easily show how it will be a step-dame to Truth; and first by disenabling us to the maintenance of what is known already.

Well knows hu who uses to consider, that our faith and knowledge thrives by exercise, as well as our limbs and complexion. Truth is compared in Scripture to a streaming fountain; if its waters flow not in a perpetual progression, they sicken into a muddy pool of conformity and tradition. A person may be a heretic in the truth; and if hu believe things only because hus pastor says so, or the Assembly so determines, without knowing other reason, though hus belief be true, yet the very truth hu holds becomes hus heresy. There is not any burden that some would gladlier post off to another than the charge and care of their religion. There be, who knows not that there be, of Protestants and professors who live and died in as arrant an implicit faith, as any lay papist of Loreto.

A wealthy person addicted to hus pleasure and to hus profits, finds religion to be a traffic so entangled, and of so many piddling accounts, that of all mysteries hu cannot skill to keep a stock going upon that trade. What should hu do? Hu would prefer to have the name to be religious, hu would rather bear up with hus neighbors in that. What does hu, therefore, but resolves to give over toiling, and to find humself out some factor to whose care and credit hu may commit the whole managing of hus religious affairs; some divine of note and estimation that must be. To hum he adheres, resigns the whole warehouse of hus religion, with all the locks and keys into hus custody; and indeed makes the very person of that one hus religion; esteems hus associating with hum a sufficient evidence and commendatory of hus own piety. So that a person may say hus religion is now no more within humself, but is become a dividual movable, and goes and comes near hum, according as that good person frequents the house. Hu entertains hum, gives hum gifts, feasts hum, lodges hum. Hus religion comes home at night, prays, is liberally supped, and sumptuously laid to sleep, rises, is saluted, and after the malmsey [wine], or some well-spiced brewage, and better breakfasted than hu whose morning appetite would have gladly fed on green figs between Bethany and Jerusalem, hus religion walks abroad at eight, and leaves hus kind entertainer in the shop trading all day without hus religion.

Another sort there be, who, when they hear that all things shall be ordered, all things regulated and settled, nothing written but what passes through the custom-house of certain publicans that have the tonnaging and the poundaging of all free-spoken truth, will straight give themselves up into your hands, make 'em and cut 'em out what religion you please. There be delights, there be recreations and jolly pastimes that will fetch the day about from sun to sun, and rock the tedious year as in a delightful dream. What need they torture their heads with that which others have taken so strictly, and so unalterably into their own purveying? These are the fruits which a dull ease and cessation of our knowledge will bring forth among the people. How goodly, and how to be wished, were such an obedient unanimity as this, what a fine conformity would it starch us all into! Doubtless a staunch and solid piece of framework, as any January could freeze together.

Nor much better will be the consequence even among the clergy themselves. It is no new thing never heard of before, for a parochial

minister, who has hus reward, and is at hus Hercules' pillars in a warm
benefice, to be easily inclinable, if hu have nothing else that may rouse
up hus studies, to finish hus circuit in an English concordance and a
topic folio, the gatherings and savings of a sober graduateship, a harmony and a catena, treading the constant round of certain common doc-
trinal heads, attended with their uses, motives, marks, and means; out
of which, as out of an alphabet or sol-fa, by forming and transforming,
joining and disjoining variously a little bookcraft, and two hours' medita-
tion, might furnish hum unspeakably to the performance of more than
a weekly charge of sermoning; not to reckon up the infinite helps of
interlinearies, breviaries, synopses, and other loitering gear.

But as for the multitude of sermons ready printed and piled up on
every text that is not difficult, our London trading St. Thomas in his
vestry, and add to boot St. Martin and St. Hugh, have not within their
hallowed limits more vendible ware of all sorts ready made; so that penury
hu never need fear of pulpit provision, having where so plenteously
to refresh hus magazine. But if hus rear and flanks be not impaled, if
hus back door be not secured by the rigid licenser, but that a bold book
may now and then issue forth and give the assault to some of hus old
collections in their trenches; it will concern hum then to keep waking,
to stand in watch, to set good guards and sentinels about hus received
opinions, to walk the round and counter-round with hus fellow inspec-
tors, fearing lest any of hus flock be seduced, who also then would be
better instructed, better exercised and disciplined. And God send that
the fear of this diligence, which must then be used, do not make us
affect the laziness of a licensing church.

For if we be sure we are in the right, and do not hold the truth
guiltily—which becomes us not—if we ourselves don't condemn our own
weak and frivolous teaching, and the people for an untaught and ir-
religious, gadding rout, what can be more fair than when a human
judicious, learned, and of a conscience, for all that we know, as good
as theirs that taught us what we know, shall not privily from house
to house, which is more dangerous, but openly by writing, publish to
the world what hus opinion is, what hus reasons, and wherefore that
which is now thought cannot be sound? Christ urged it as the way to
justify himself that he preached in public; yet writing is more public
than preaching; and more easy to refutation, if need be, there being
so many whose business and profession merely it is, to be the cham-
pions of truth; which if they neglect, what can be imputed but their
sloth or inability?

Thus much we are hindered and disinured by this course of licensing toward the true knowledge of what we seem to know. For how much

it hurts and hinders the licensers themselves in the calling of their ministry, more than any secular employment, if they will discharge that office as they ought, so that of necessity they must neglect either the one duty or the other, I insist not, because it is a particular, but leave it to their own conscience, how they will decide it there.

There is yet behind of what I purposed to lay open, the incredible loss and detriment that this plot of licensing puts us to. More than if some enemy at sea should stop up all our havens and ports and creeks, it hinders and retards the importation of our richest merchandise, truth. No, it was first established and put in practice by anti-Christian malice and mystery, on set purpose to extinguish, if it were possible, the light of Reformation, and to settle falsehood; little differing from that policy in which the Turk upholds hus Al-Koran by the prohibition of printing. 'Tis not denied, but gladly confessed, we are to send our thanks and vows to Heaven, louder than most of nations, for that great measure of truth which we enjoy, especially in those main points between us and the Pope, with hus appurtenances the prelates; but hu who thinks we are to pitch our tent here, and have attained the utmost prospect of Reformation that the mortal glass wherein we contemplate can show us, till we come to beatific vision, that person by this very opinion declares that hu is yet far short of truth.

Truth indeed came once into the world with her divine Master, and was a perfect shape most glorious to look on. But when he ascended, and his apostles after him were laid asleep, then straight arose a wicked race of deceivers, who, as that story goes of the Egyptian Typhon with his conspirators, how they dealt with the good Osiris, took the virgin Truth, hewed her lovely form into a thousand pieces, and scattered them to the four winds. From that time ever since, the sad friends of Truth, such as dared appear, imitating the careful search that Isis made for the mangled body of Osiris, went up and down gathering limb by limb still as they could find them. We have not yet found them all, Lords and Commons, nor ever shall do, till her Master's second coming. He shall bring together every joint and member, and shall mold them into an immortal feature of loveliness and perfection. Suffer not these licensing prohibitions to stand at every place of opportunity, forbidding and disturbing them that continue seeking, that continue to do our obsequies to the torn body of our martyred saint.

We boast our light; but if we look not wisely on the sun itself, it smites us into darkness. Who can discern those planets that are often combust, and those stars of brightest magnitude that rise and set with the sun, until the opposite motion of their orbs bring them to such a place in the firmament, where they may be seen evening or morning?

The light which we have gained, was given us, not to be ever staring on, but by it to discover onward things more remote from our knowledge. It is not the unfrocking of a priest, the unmitering of a bishop, and the removing hum from the Presbyterian shoulders that will make us a happy nation; no, if other things as great in the Church, and in the rule of life both economical and political, be not looked into and reformed, we have looked so long upon the blaze that Zwinglius and Calvin have beaconed up to us, that we are stark blind.

There are those who perpetually complain of schisms and sects, and make it such a calamity that any person dissents from their maxims. 'Tis their own pride and ignorance which causes the disturbing, who neither will hear with meekness, nor can convince, yet all must be suppressed which is not found in their syntagma. They are the troublers, they are the dividers of unity, who neglect and don't permit others to unite those dissevered pieces which are yet wanting to the body of Truth. To be still searching what we don't know by what we know, still closing up truth to truth as we find it (for all her body is homogeneal and proportional), this is the golden rule in theology as well as in arithmetic, and makes up the best harmony in a church; not the forced and outward union of cold and neutral and inwardly divided minds.

Lords and Commons of England, consider what nation it is where you are, and of which you are the governors; a nation not slow and dull, but of a quick, ingenious, and piercing spirit, acute to invent, subtle and sinewy to discourse, not beneath the reach of any point the highest that human capacity can soar to. Therefore the studies of learning in hus deepest sciences have been so ancient and so eminent among us, that writers of good antiquity and ablest judgment have been persuaded that even the school of Pythagoras and the Persian wisdom, took beginning from the old philosophy of this island. And that wise and civil Roman, Julius Agricola, who governed once here for Caesar, preferred the natural wits of Britain before the labored studies of the French. Nor is it for nothing that the grave and frugal Transylvanian sends out yearly from as far as the mountainous borders of Russia and beyond the Hercynian wilderness, not their youth but their staid persons, to learn our language and our theologic arts.

Yet that which is above all this, the favor and the love of Heaven, we have great argument to think in a peculiar manner propitious and propending towards us. Why else was this nation chosen before any other, that out of it as out of Zion should be proclaimed and sounded forth the first tidings and trumpet of Reformation to all Europe? And had it not been the obstinate perverseness of our prelates against the divine and admirable spirit of Wyclif, to suppress him as a schismatic and innovator, perhaps neither the Bohemian Huss and Jerome (of Prague), no, nor the name of Luther, or of Calvin, had been ever known; the glory of reforming all our neighbors had been completely ours. But now, as our obdurate clergy have with violence demeaned the matter, we are become hitherto the latest and the most backward scholars, of whom God offered to have made us the teachers.

Now once again by all concurrence of signs, and by the general instinct of holy and devout people, as they daily and solemnly express their thoughts, God is decreeing to begin some new and great period in hus Church, even to the reforming of Reformation itself. What does hu then but reveal humself to hus servants, and, as hus manner is, first to hus English? I say as hus manner is, first to us, though we mark not the method of hus counsels, and are unworthy. Behold now this vast city, a city of refuge, the mansion house of liberty, encompassed and surrounded with hus protection. The shop of war has not there more anvils and hammers waking, to fashion out the plates and instruments of armed justice in defense of beleaguered truth, than there are pens and heads there, sitting by their studious lamps, musing, searching, revolving new notions and ideas wherewith to present, as with their homage and their fealty, the approaching Reformation; others as fast reading, trying all things, assenting to the force of reason and convincement.

What could a person require more from a nation so pliant and so prone to seek after knowledge? What lacks there to such a towardly and pregnant soil, but wise and faithful laborers, to make a knowing people, a nation of prophets, of sages, and of worthies? We reckon more than five months yet to harvest; there need not be five weeks, had we but eyes to lift up; the fields are white already. Where there is much desire to learn, there of necessity will be much arguing, much writing, many opinions; for opinion in good persons is but knowledge in the making. Under these fantastic terrors of sect and schism, we wrong the earnest and zealous thirst after knowledge and understanding which God has stirred up in this city.

What some lament of, we rather should rejoice at, should rather praise this pious forwardness among people, to reassume the ill-deputed care of their religion into their own hands again. A little generous prudence, a little forbearance of one another, and some grain of charity might win all these diligences to join and unite into one general and friendly search after truth; could we but forego this prelatical tradition of crowding free consciences and Christian liberties into canons and precepts of humanity. I doubt not, if some great and worthy stranger should come among us, wise to discern the mold and temper of a people, and how to govern it, observing the high hopes and aims, the diligent alacrity of our extended thoughts and reasonings in the pursuance of truth and freedom, but that hu would cry out as Pyrrhus did, admiring the Roman docility and courage, "If such were my Epirots, I would not despair the greatest design that could be attempted to make a church or kingdom happy."

Yet these are the people cried out against for schismatics and sectaries; as if, while the Temple of the Lord was building, some cutting, some squaring the marble, others hewing the cedars, there should be a sort of irrational person who could not consider there must be many schisms and many dissections made in the quarry and in the timber, before the house of God can be built. And when every stone is laid artfully together, it cannot be united into a continuity, it can but be contiguous in this world; neither can every piece of the building be of one form; but rather the perfection consists in this, that out of many moderate varieties and friendly dissimilitudes that are not vastly disproportional, arises the goodly and the graceful symmetry that commends the whole pile and structure.

Let us, therefore, be more considerate builders, more wise in spiritual architecture, when great reformation is expected. For now the time seems come, when Moses, the great prophet, may sit in heaven rejoicing to see that memorable and glorious wish of his fulfilled, when not only our seventy elders, but all the Lord's people, are become prophets. No marvel then though some people, and some good people too, perhaps, but young in goodness, as Joshua then was, envy them. They fret, and out of their own weakness are in agony, for fear that these divisions and subdivisions will undo us. The adversary again applauds, and waits the hour when they have branched themselves out, says hu, small enough into parties and partitions, then will be our time. Fool! hu sees not the firm root out of which we all grow, though into branches; nor will beware until hu see our small divided maniples cutting through at every angle of hus ill-united and unwieldy brigade. And that we are to hope better of all these supposed sects and schisms, and that we shall not need that solicitude, honest perhaps, though over-timorous, of them that vex in this behalf, but shall laugh in the end at those malicious applauders of our differences, I have these reasons to persuade me.

First, when a city shall be as it were besieged and blocked about, its navigable river infested, inroads and incursions round, defiance and battle oft rumored to be marching up even to its walls and suburb trenches; that then the people, or the greater part, more than at other times, wholly taken up with the study of highest and most important matters to be reformed, should be disputing, reasoning, reading, inventing, discoursing, even to a rarity and admiration, things not before discoursed or written of, argues first a singular good will, contentedness and confidence in your prudent foresight, and safe government, Lords and Commons; and from thence derives itself to a gallant bravery and well grounded contempt of their enemies, as if there were no small number of as great spirits among us, as hus was, who, when Rome was nigh besieged by Hannibal, being in the city, bought that piece of ground at no cheap rate on which Hannibal himself encamped his own regiment.

Next, it is a lively and cheerful presage of our happy success and victory. For as in a body, when the blood is fresh, the spirits pure and vigorous not only to vital but to rational faculties, and those in the most acute and the most pert operations of wit and subtlety, it argues in what good plight and constitution the body is; so when the cheerfulness of the people is so sprightly up, as that it has, not only that with which to guard well its own freedom and safety, but to spare, and to bestow upon the most solid and most sublime points of controversy and new invention, it betokens us not degenerated nor drooping to a fatal decay, but casting off the old and wrinkled skin of corruption to outlive these pangs, and wax young again, entering the glorious ways of truth and prosperous virtue, destined to become great and honorable in these latter ages.

I think I see in my mind a noble and puissant nation rousing humself like a strong person after sleep, and shaking hus invincible locks. I think I see hum as an eagle mewing hus mighty youth, and kindling hus undazzled eyes at the full midday beam; purging and unscaling hus long-abused sight at the fountain itself of heavenly radiance; while the whole noise of timorous and flocking birds, with those also that love the twilight, flutter about, amazed at what hu means, and in their envious gabble would prognosticate a year of sects and schisms.

What should you do then, should you suppress all this flowery crop of knowledge and new light sprung up and yet springing daily in this city? Should you set an oligarchy of twenty engrossers over it, to bring a famine upon our minds again, when we shall know nothing but what is measured to us by their bushel? Believe it, Lords and Commons, they who counsel you to such a suppressing, do as good as bid you suppress yourselves; and I will soon show how.

If it be desired to know the immediate cause of all this free writing and free speaking, there cannot be assigned a truer than your own mild and free and humane government. It is the liberty, Lords and Commons, which your own valorous and happy counsels have purchased us, liberty which is the nurse of all great wits. This is that which has rarefied and enlightened our spirits like the influence of heaven; this is that which has enfranchised, enlarged, and lifted up our apprehensions degrees above themselves. You cannot make us now less capable, less knowing, less eagerly pursuing of the truth, unless you first make yourselves, that made us so, less the lovers, less the founders of our true liberty. We can grow ignorant again, brutish, formal, and slavish, as you found us; but you then must first become that which you cannot be, oppressive, arbitrary, and tyrannous, as they were from whom you have freed us. That our hearts are now more capacious, our thoughts more erected to the search and expectation of greatest and most exact things, is the issue of your own virtue propagated in us. You cannot suppress that unless you reinforce an abrogated and merciless law, that parents may despatch at will their own children. And who shall then stick closest to you, and excite others? Not hu who takes up arms for coat and conduct, and hus four nobles of Danegelt [taxes]. Although I dispraise not the defense of just immunities, yet love my peace better, if that were all. Give me the liberty to know, to utter, and to argue freely according to conscience, above all liberties.

What would be best advised, then, if it be found so hurtful and so unequal to suppress opinions for the newness, or the unsuitableness to a customary acceptance, will not be my task to say. I only shall repeat what I have learned from one of your own honorable number, a right noble and pious Lord, who, had he not sacrificed his life and fortunes to the Church and Commonwealth, we had not now missed and bewailed a worthy and undoubted patron of this argument. You know him I am sure; yet I for honor's sake, and may it be eternal to him, shall name him, the Lord Brooke. He, writing of Episcopacy, and by the way treating of sects and schisms, left you his vote, or rather now the last words of his dying charge (which I know will ever be of dear and honored regard with you) so full of meekness and breathing charity that next to his last testament, who bequeathed love and peace to his disciples, I cannot call to mind where I have read or heard words more mild and peaceful. He there exhorts us to hear with patience and humility those, however they be miscalled, that desire to live purely, in such a use of God's ordinances as the best guidance of their conscience gives them, and to tolerate them, though in some disconformity to ourselves. The book itself will tell us more at large, being published to the world and dedicated to the Parliament by him who, both for his life and for his death, deserves that what advice he left be not laid by without perusal.

And now the time in special is, by privilege to write and speak what may help to the further discussing of matters in agitation. The temple of Janus with his two controversal faces might now not unsignificantly be set open, as if for war. And though all the winds of doctrine were let loose to play upon the earth, so Truth be in the field, we do injuriously by licensing and prohibiting to misdoubt her strength. Let her and Falsehood grapple; who ever knew Truth put to the worse, in a free and open encounter? Her confuting is the best and surest suppressing. Hu who hears what praying there is for light and clearer knowledge to be sent down among us, would think of other matters to be constituted beyond the discipline of Geneva, framed and fabricked already to our hands.

Yet when the new light which we beg for shines in upon us, there are who envy and oppose, if it come not first in at their casements. What a collusion is this, when we are exhorted by the wise person to use diligence, to seek for wisdom as for hidden treasures early and late, that another order shall enjoin us to know nothing but by statute. When a person has been laboring the hardest labor in the deep mines of knowledge, has furnished out hus findings in all their equipage, drawn forth hus reasons as it were a battle ranged, scattered and defeated all objections in hus way, calls out hus adversary into the plain, offers hum the advantage of wind and sun, if hu please; only that hu may try the matter by dint of argument, for hus opponents then to skulk, to lay ambushments, to keep a narrow bridge of licensing where the challenger should pass, though it be valor enough in soldiership, is but weakness and cowardice in the wars of Truth.

For who knows not that Truth is strong, next to the Almighty? She needs no policies, nor strategems, nor licensings to make her victorious—those are the shifts and the defenses that error uses against her power. Give her but room, and do not bind her when she sleeps, for then she speaks not true, as the old Proteus did, who spake oracles only when he was caught and bound, but rather she turns herself into all shapes except her own, and perhaps tunes her voice according to the time, as Micaiah did before Ahab, until she be adjured into her own likeness.

Yet it is not impossible that she may have more shapes than one. What else is all that rank of things indifferent, wherein Truth may be on this side, or on the other, without being unlike herself? What but a vain shadow else is the abolition of those ordinances, that hand-writing nailed to the cross; what great purchase is this Christian liberty which Paul so often boasts of? His doctrine is, that hu who eats, or eat from another, though it be not in fundamentals; and through our forwardness to suppress, and our backwardness to recover any enthralled piece of truth out of the grip of custom, we care not to keep truth separated from truth, which is the fiercest rent and disunion of all. We do not see that while we still affect by all means a rigid external formality, we may as soon fall again into a gross conforming stupidity, a stark and dead congealment of "wood, and hay, and stubble" forced and frozen together, which is more to the sudden degenerating of a church than many subdichotomies of petty schisms.

Not that I can think well of every light separation, or that all in a church is to be expected gold and silver and precious stones. It is not possible for people to sever the wheat from the tares, the good fish from the other fry; that must be the angels' ministry at the end of mortal things. Yet if all cannot be of one mind—as who looks they should be?—this doubtless is more wholesome, more prudent, and more Christian, that many be tolerated, rather than all compelled. I do not mean tolerated popery and open superstition, which, as it extirpates all religions and civil supremacies, so itself should be extirpate, provided first that all charitable and compassionate means be used to win and regain the weak and the misled; that also which is impious or evil absolutely, either against faith or manners, no law can possibly permit, that does not intend to unlaw itself; but those neighboring differences, or rather indifferences, are what I speak of, whether in some point of doctrine or of discipline, which though they may be many, yet need not interrupt the unity of spirit, if we could but find among us the bond of peace.

In the meanwhile, if anyone would write and bring hus helpful hand to the slow-moving Reformation which we labor under, if truth have spoken to hum before others, or but seemed at least to speak, who has so bejesuited us that we should trouble that person with asking license to do so worthy a deed, and not consider this, that if it come to prohibiting, there is not anything more likely to be prohibited than truth itself; whose first appearance to our eyes bleared and dimmed with prejudice and custom, is more unsightly and unplausible than many errors, even as the person is of many a great one slight and contemptible to see to? And what do they tell us vainly of new opinions, when this very opinion of theirs, that none must be heard but whom they like, is the worst and newest opinion of all others; and is the chief cause why sects and schisms do so much abound, and true knowledge is kept at a distance from us; besides yet a greater danger which is in it? For when God shakes a kingdom with strong and healthful commotions to a general reforming, it is not untrue that many sectaries and false teachers are then busiest in seducing; but yet more true it is that God then raises to hus own work persons of rare abilities, and more than common industry, not only to look back and revise what has been taught heretofore, but to gain further and go on, some new enlightened steps in the discovery of truth.

For such is the order of God's enlightening hus church, to dispense and deal out by degrees hus beam, so as our earthly eyes may best sustain it. Neither is God appointed and confined, where and out of what place these hus chosen shall be first heard to speak: for hu sees not as a person sees, chooses not as a person chooses, lest we should devote ourselves again to set places, and assemblies, and outward callings of humans; planting our faith one while in the old Convocation house, and another while in the Chapel at Westminster; when all the faith and religion that shall be there canonized, is not sufficient without plain convincement and the charity of patient instruction, to supple the least bruise of conscience, to edify the meanest Christian who desires those who, not contented with stale receipts, are able to manage and set forth new positions to the world. And were they but as the dust and cinders of our feet, so long as in that notion they may yet serve to polish and brighten the armory of Truth, even for that respect they were not utterly to be cast away. But if they be of those whom God has fitted for the special use of these times with eminent and ample gifts—and those perhaps neither among the priests, nor among the pharisees—and we in the haste of a precipitant zeal shall make no distinction, but resolve to stop their mouths because we fear they come with new and dangerous opinions (as we commonly forejudge them before we understand them); no less than woe to us while, thinking thus to defend the Gospel, we are found the persecutors.

There have been not a few since the beginning of this [Long] Parliament, both of the Presbytery and others, who by their unlicensed books, to the contempt of an *Imprimatur,* first broke that triple ice clung about our hearts, and taught the people to see day. I hope that none of those were the persuaders to renew upon us this bondage which they themselves have wrought so much good by contemning. But if neither the check that Moses gave to young Joshua, nor the countermand which our Savior gave to young John, who was so ready to prohibit those whom he thought unlicensed, be not enough to admonish our elders how unacceptable to God their testy mood of prohibiting is; if neither their own remembrance what evil has abounded in the church by this obstruction of licensing, and what good they themselves have begun by transgressing it, be not enough, but that they will persuade and execute the most Dominican part of the Inquisition over us, and are already with one foot in the stirrup so active at suppressing, it would be no unequal distribution, in the first place, to suppress the suppressors themselves; whom the change of their condition has puffed up, more than their late experience of harder times has made wise.

And as for regulating the press, let no one think to have the honor of advising you better than yourselves have done in that order published next before this, "that no book be printed, unless the printer's and the author's name, or at least the printer's, be registered." Those which otherwise come forth, if they be found mischievous and libellous, the fire and the executioner will be the timeliest and the most effectual remedy that human prevention can use. For this authentic Spanish policy of licensing books, if I have said anything, will prove the most unlicensed book itself within a short while; and was the immediate image of a Star Chamber decree to that purpose made in those very times when that Court did the rest of those its pious works, for which it is now fallen from the stars with Lucifer. Whereby you may guess what kind of state prudence, what love of the people, what care of religion or good manners there was at the contriving, although with singular hypocrisy it pretended to bind books to their good behavior. And how it got the upper hand of your precedent order so well constituted before, if we may believe those persons whose profession gives them cause to inquire most, it may be doubted there was in it the fraud of some old patentees and monopolizers in the trade of bookselling; who under pretense of the poor in their Company not to be defrauded, and the just retaining of each person hus several copy[rights] (which God forbid should be gainsaid) brought diverse glossing colors to the House, which were indeed but colors, and serving to no end except it be to exercise a superiority over their neighbors; persons who do not, therefore, labor in an honest profession to which learning is indebted, that they should be made other people's vassals. Another end is thought was aimed at by some of them in procuring by petition this Order, that having power in their hands, malignant books might the easier escape abroad, as the event shows.

But of these sophisms and refutations of merchandise I skill not. This I know, that errors in good government and in a bad are equally almost incident; for what magistrate may not be misinformed and much the sooner, if liberty of printing be reduced into the power of a few? But to redress willingly and speedily what has been erred, and in highest authority to esteem a plain advertisement more than others have done a sumptuous bribe, is a virtue, honored Lords and Commons, answerable to your highest actions, and whereof none can participate but greatest and wisest persons.